A DEVON ANTHOLOGY

A Collection of New Writings
from the Wordquest Devon Project

GW00692221

a Wordquestdevon commission

A Devon Anthology
A Collection of New Writings
from the Wordquest Devon Project

Editor: Sarah Cobley

Sub Editor: Susannah Lash

Printed by: ImprintDigital.com

Design by: Joe Pieczenko

Published 2012: Aune Head Arts

www.wordquestdevon.info

ISBN 978-0-9566114-1-3

Contents

Introduction

As Creative Producer for Wordquest Devon I have had the pleasure of travelling around the county meeting people young and old, published writers, those who have never written and everything in between.

Wordquest Devon engaged the public in explorations of Devon's literary heritage through the development of new skills, new writing, creative explorations in words and new investigations of the natural environment. This book is a collection of the new writings created during the project from commissioned writers, young poetry competition winners and people who may have stumbled upon a book in progress and added a sentence.

Wordquest Devon began life as a response to the 'questing' themes of the Cultural Olympiad, and retained many of these playful and game-playing aspects throughout. It was a project led by Aune Head Arts with partners Cyprus Well, Devon Libraries (Devon County Council), and the University of Exeter.

Funding support for this project was generously provided by Devon County Council, The Heritage Lottery Fund, Arts Council England, South Devon Coastal Local Action Group, Team Devon and the Greater Dartmoor Local Enterprise Action Fund. In-kind support was provided by Aune Head Arts, Cyprus Well, Devon Libraries and the University of Exeter.

Sarah Cobley

POETRY

POETRY

It is no easy thing, in evoking the spirit or even the appearance of a place, to push through beyond the difficulties that can beset writing about landscape and the natural world. Think of those poems whose success is curtailed either by their failure to match the natural grandeur to which they witness (Dartmoor is a case in point), or in which the view is spoilt by cliché or the writer's too obvious grafting of personal feeling.

All to the good, then, that the poems here aim to do justice to the active imagination. Between them they show an attractive variety of approach, both formally and in terms of focus: Fiona Benson's taut lines and telling preciseness, springing off from closely defined locations; a poem constructed by a class from St Catherine's Primary School, Heathfield, working together; a children's competition on the theme of a favourite place; Ralph Hoyte's free-booting 'Walk-Poem', and his declared interest in musicality and voice; and a poem by Alicia Grace (a sestina with a relaxed view of line lengths) that takes a mobile library as its point of departure.

The common ground is, of course, that of Devon, as well as an awareness of the ways in which the past infuses the present – but also the virtue of paying proper attention to what a given place has to offer, if the observer is sufficiently alert. This refreshment of attentiveness, along with the discovery of language that can enact it, represents an abiding challenge for all those whose quests are conducted in the medium of words. As the American writer Marge Piercy has put it: 'There are no poetic subjects, only subjects to which we pay the right kind of attention.'

Lawrence Sail

Thanks first and foremost to Wordquest for enabling this work through their commission, especially to Sarah Cobley; also to all at Cyprus Well, who managed the project, especially Alex Cluness, Tracey Guiry and David Woolley.

Thanks also to the guides at Kent's Cavern; Mrs Judith Lewis, warden of Ashburton Parish Church; Rachel McCarthy, for her support and help with tide times; Damian Furniss; and in particular to Kerri Walsh and Déborah Martín Duarte for help with Isla-care.

Thanks to Alice Oswald, for mentoring these poems.

I went to Plymouth intending to write about the old RAF base and the Sunderland flying boats. I ended up writing about the submarines. The poem is nonetheless dedicated to my father, David Benson.

Special thanks, as always, to David-Antoine Williams for his unendingly patient editorial advice, and to James and Isla Meredith for helping me find the poems and putting up with me while I wrote them. These poems are dedicated with love to the three of you.

Fiona Benson

DUMNONIA

Fiona Benson

DUMNONIA

Fiona Benson

Contents

I wanted the woods
and the woods' corollary –
squirrel hoard,
seeding of teeth,

stag-antler, microlith –
but when the tide pulls back
to its lowest ebb
all that's left

of the waterlogged forest –
its shoals of acorn
and drifts of leaf,
the shut-up cist of an egg –

are these dank, eroded beds
of peat-stained oak, pocked
with vanished colonies of whelk
and halfway troughed in sand.

How will I get beyond
the let down of these slabs,
how will I find my way back
to the woods,

its dim snares and drowned roots,
the ghost of an owl
still sharking in the treetops,
circling its flooded roost?

Cave Bear

You snarl in the lintel
and hold your ground,
your lower jaw blown out,
the roof of your mouth
vented and rough

constellate
of bone-shard, tooth.
Set at your neck
is the muzzle of a cub,
its crooked skull.

Four hundred thousand years
embedded in this cave:
drip of lime,
dirt in the trench
of your rotted tongue,

the hollow of your brain
cased in stone
till you are a vault
for the one clear thought
of your life:

the cub is dead.
You show your teeth
as the massive slab
of your heart
gives way.

Clapper Bridge

Clappers: quarried flats
laid like tableboards
over stacked supports
and colonised by lichens, moss.

You love the coppery run
of the stream, its scatter of insects
ringed in brightness
the single, slate-finned fish

but what you want
is the way light projects
on the underside of these granite slabs
with a soft, ravelling mobility

what you want is waterlight,
that dance, that luminous flux
and the fraction's shift
in the bedrock of the moor

that puts you on course
with the barrowbuilders
shouldering along the lych way
heavy-footed at the fording place.

Urn-Burial

A dozen jars, furred
with dirt, a piece of slate
across each throat

and thought, at first,
to be set for resonance,
a slight and subtle antiphon.

But what of this residue,
this rosin,
these thin hearts sleeping,

each occulted in a separate vase?
We slid them back unmarked.
Confess their pulse

in the unstill walls of the church
and you make room for the exiled dead,
crusaders buried abroad,

their quarried hearts
sent home to roost,
like the martins stowed

in their own dull jars
of spit and mud,
querulous under the roof.

For Temperance Lloyd

Next time I'll walk the old cart route to the drop.
For now it's enough to see the castle walls
grown derelict with trees and the fosse dammed up
with leaves. The fort's long gone and the keep
but the gatehouse squats on still, red-bricked sentry
of the city road. You were brought through this gate for trial.
Now it's nailed across with a mock portcullis
and the doves are frightened from the courtyards and towers
by plastic decoys of owls that spin above the ramparts,
and which I take at first for heads.
My heart is a sad swinging in its cage.
You are a thin thought turning over the walls
in a grey wind, transparent, spider-weight.
I'd have you angry and impenitent and brave.
I'd have you fly from the drop in the shape of a rook,
its rag-and-bone, its bloodshot eye. Instead
you're this palsied old woman in a stained shift
and shawl, your hair thin as carded wool,
hugging your breasts in the cold. On trial
you swore you'd been a cat, that a demon sucked
your private parts, that you pricked and harmed
that man's sick wife. Now you miss the chase
of the Bideford coast but are pleased overall
to be looked at, riding in this cart, when all
your life you've been invisible and walked.

Devonport

Will he make a covenant with thee?
Wilt thou take him for a servant for ever?

Job 41:4

Holstered in the Tamar
the low-slung bolts
of submarines come home.

Each breached hood
looks like part of the wharf –
black pontoon or tidal berth

and breathes no word
of its underwater heft,
its airlocks and vaults,

its sintered, nuclear core.
Pray for our fathers on leave
who, in the unstable crucible

of sleep, crawl
through drowning rooms
of war and sorrow.

Pray for the difficult undoing
of each shining, fissioned load,
the slow decay of isotopes.

Would that the old wars were done with.
The sea is still a torpedo-path,
an Armageddon road.

Year 6 pupils from St Catherine's Primary School in Heathfield took part in a writing workshop at Stover Country Park using the Ted Hughes Poetry Trail as a starting point for their inspiration to create their class poem.

Maze Of Life
St Catherine's Primary School

MAZE OF LIFE

St Catherine's Primary School

Towering trees touch the clear sky with icy fingers
Crowding like an army of soldiers
A glistening glimmer of water glimpsed through
Motionless trees standing to attention
Pale sun pushes its way through the canopy
Weak spotlights filtering through branches - dappled shade.

A maze of life
White figures float in the frozen air
Seagulls squabble as they duck and dive
Swans as white as snow
Fly sharp as a dart then
Glide – elegant, peaceful, swift, silent
Graceful, gently caressing the water
Beady eyes as dark as midnight.

Cormorant silhouetted still as a statue against the icy sky
Feathers blowing in the breeze
Coot, flaming eyes like embers in a fire
Iridescent metallic mallards.

Ripples chase the sun like a shadow
Rainbow circles glisten in the calm water
Reflections like magical illusions.

Year 6 St Catherine's Primary School

A Poetry Competition for Children and Young People

Inspired by National Poetry Day, Wordquest Devon invited children and young people to celebrate their special place in Devon.

My Favourite Place in Devon

a poetry competition for children and young people

MY FAVOURITE
PLACE IN DEVON

A Poetry Competition for Children and Young People

One day we walked past the apples and cows
To the deep dark Pridhamsleigh cave
I had my mud suit helmet and torch
But was I feeling brave?

Down the hole I slipped and slithered
I felt something in my sock
I shone my torch to find my feet
Deep in mud… what a shock!

With no wind the air is still
Under the rocks we crawl
In the spooky dark blackness
There's nothing to see at all.

We make our way to the lake
Past giant growing stalagmites
The rocks are covered in a squishy clay
Hanging overhead are pale stalactites.

I wriggle like a worm
Through narrow passage ways
Into the Coal Hole I was dropped
It seems like I was there for days.

I emerged to a blinding flash of light
The warm sunshine on my face
With great big muddy smiles
Down to the river we race.

Toby Rowe, Age 7

Plymouth Aquarium

Pipefish swim around
Long eels slide about
Young fish swim with parents
Monsters of the sea
Orange red and blue
Ugly creatures too,
Tentacles and tails
Huge fish and whales,
Amazing sea life
Quiet fish
Under the water
A ray swims
Round puffer fish puff up
Inside rocks crabs crawl
Unique sea life
My favourite place is Plymouth Aquarium

Harry Woolfenden, Age 8

My Garden

Mummy lets me plant flowers and vegetables
Yellow primroses and daffodil.

Gardening in the sun
Around our garden there are lots of beautiful birds
Rain I can jump in puddles
Den for playing in
Exciting
Newts on the grass and in the stream.

Imogen Sky Tucker, Age 7

Like a big green umbrella
Sheltering the mossy woodland ground
The damp musty smell, like old wellie boots fills the air
Squelching mud oozing from under my boots
As we scramble along the path.

Velvet blackberries nestling in hedgerows
A brown and gold palace of leaves
An autumn breeze carries the leaves
Like confetti falling from the heavens
Ready to crackle under foot
Bright red berries glistening under a blanket of snow
Waiting for spring to come.

A green forest canopy
Sunlight, streaming through
A stained glass window appearing on the floor
Mellow yellow daffodils among the blanket of snowdrops
Giggles and laughter
The snapping of twigs as secret dens are made.

My woodland wonder.

Kieran Brookes, Age 9

In My Garden

In my garden on my swing, is where I sit and I am king
King of my head, King of my thoughts, King of my life
In my garden it has all sorts.

In my garden on my trampoline,
Holds fun 'til I am one hundred and fifteen
I jump, I fly, I flip, I spring
Gallons of fun it does bring

In my garden on a hot summers day
When the clouds are not grey
We get the hose and we spray
Slipping through the soaked grass
Move inside? I will pass

In my garden on a snowy winters day
Wrapped up so warm so I'm ok
Snow angels, one foot deep
Sledging in fields so steep
Igloo making, snowball fighting
Been having fun since dawn this morning

In my garden it holds memories
The land and the activities
I swung on that swing on my third party
In my garden I roam free
In my garden is the place to be.

Tabitha Evans, Age 10

Church Path in Upton Hellions

Hazel, spindle an oak tree
Badgers, foxes and little yellow bees
As I walk down the path
this is what I see

There's hedgerows along the side
Holes where badgers hide
Mushrooms growing out the mud
And in the spring there's busting buds
Close to woodlands far from town
Green looking up and red looking down
I sing this poem as I go down Church Path

Eva Casey, Age 8

Fire on the Common

Blackened fingers scorched and powdery, point up towards the sky
As if blaming the clouds for Tuesday's disaster

All the saplings and shrubs are charcoal now,
Dull, black, crumbling charcoal

Pointing to the blue sky and to the clouds that break before me
to let through the sun – its glorious rays make the ashes smoke

and the stubs on inky black sparkle and glitter
I move through the cremated sticks and plants
And I wonder why the sky released its bolt of electricity
Left us nothing but the blackened fingers pointing to the sky

Lilygrace Hellier, Age 13

As the wind blows,
Hedges cling on to their cliff top home

As the wind blows,
The sea licks the sand savouring the taste

As the wind blows,
Pebbles overturn on the rocky seabed

As the wind blows,
Grass bows at its mighty power

As the wind blows,
Sheep bleat as they are bowled over

As the wind blows,
Roof tiles scream before they shatter

As the wind blows,
Sand is flecked up in my face

As the wind blows,
Salty air reaches my nose

As the wind blows,
I hear the echo of laughter

As the wind blows on through Challaborough

Catherine Rowland, Age 11

My Garden

My garden,
It may not seem very much,
But if you knew it like I do you'd know why it's special,
The sharp, spiky gravel stones that dig into your feet above the chocolate brown soil,
Birds chirping to the tone of a slight breeze as soft as a pillow

My garden,
Grass ripped and torn,
From the sport contested by competitive brothers,
And the running and sprinting that makes me muddy and sweaty
But despite getting cold and wet I never want to stop

My garden,
Surrounded by dull coloured crumbling walls hit by numerous balls,
The place of parties that go on all night,
Where Frisbees are thrown to my dog,

My garden,
My place,
My garden,
My memories

Liam Travers, Age 13

That Old Tree

That tree that I see every time I pass that house
That house I used to live in
At the bottom of the field
At my favourite place in Devon.

The smell of the bark and the texture of the leaves
The green, green leaves
Made me feel like I was in a rainforest
Made me know I was somewhere special.

Hiding and running to that tree
Hiding from my friends and running in circles
Remembering those days being little and young
Remembering feeding the horses and watching them gallop.

All from that tree

That old tree I used to climb all the day
That old tree I used to read at
How I would run everyday to it
Being sheltered from the rain
By the leaves hanging over me.

As the snow would come down
As my brother would throw snowballs at me
My special tree would be my shield
My tiny hill surrounding it would be a slide of ice as the ice fell.

I have moved from that house
I have moved away from my favourite place
As I pass the house in the morning
As I look and remember all the good times I have had at that tree.

Remembering I had some things hidden in a hole
Remembering that I had forgotten everything hidden there
How I would always find new places to hide things
How I miss my favourite place in Devon.

Becky Birt-Mitchell, Age 14

No Place Like Home

Dawn blooms, scattering beams across the waking sky,
To gently break another morrow and signal the darks goodbye,
Beauty uncovered by the sun's blaze, the blaze that waned the night,
Exposing the stretch of nature's finest works; a truly spectacular sight.

The chorus of frantic caws and chirps that sound the morning song,
Sing merrily with mirth and vigour, goading others to sing along.
The quiescent sound of the flowing stream gently trickles near,
All lulls your mind into calmness, as it sounds into your ear.

The meadow is filled with stirring buds, colours of pink, red and blue,
Calmly spread across the grass, adorning the hedgerows too,
The breeze does softly blow, a crisp yet soothing draft,
Swaying low tree branches that hold more detail than an artist's craft.

You must enjoy it while you can, this wondrous gift of ours,
For we will soon bid farewell, as the sun is overpowered,
The clock ticks and hours pass, turning dawn back into the dusk,
The moon returns to take her place, receiving the skies as she must.

And so it seems the light has brought another blissful day,
Giving warmth and life to earth, whilst showing her display.
This privilege we bear is great, so let us make it known,
The honour we possess in saying, how proud we are to call Devon our home.

Lottie Walker, Age 15

The Wave Poem

The wave is coming, the wave is coming
It rises and rises like a lumbering beast
The wave has come, the wave has come
It picks me up like a great blue giant
The wave is here, the wave is here
It roars behind me like a hungry lion
The wave is angry, the wave is angry
It bucks and it sways like a wild mare
The wave is dying, the wave is dying
I turn and I weave like a humming bird
The wave is dead, the wave is dead
I grind to a halt like an exhausted runner
The wave is gone, the wave is gone
So I paddle out for another go

Sam Marshall, Age 14

SALAMI-SLICING THE INTERNAL LANDSCAPE (or: from Salcombe to Dartmouth on the SW Coastpath) is a long declamatory walk-poem for two voices (male and female). One is that of The Wandering Man (mine), and the female voice is that of The Green Sea Witch, who joined me on the walk.

I took a train from Bristol Temple Meads to Plymouth. From Plymouth I took the no. 95 bus to Kingsbridge then walked to Salcombe where I over-nighted at the YH. On Day 1 I took the ferry over the estuary (actually a 'ria') and dawdled along to Start Point, 'dawdling' being an essential part of composition. I wild-camped the first night high on Start Point, in the only place protected from a fierce wind. On Day 2 I walked past Hallsands – where a community slid into the sea – and on to Torcross, Slapton Sands and Slapton itself. Slapton Sands was the 'theatre' (literally) for Operation Tiger, a simulated landing in preparation for the D-Day Normandy Landings of the 2nd World War. More soldiers lost their lives in the simulation than in the actual landings. On Day 3 I wandered on, up towards Dartmouth, then on the last day I crossed the estuary, took a bus to Paignton and a train back home to Bristol.

In the poem, as in much of my work nowadays, I attempt to compress 'words' until, like a hypernova, they collapse under their own weight, or, as with the Hadron collider, I pepper them with word particles and see what results. And of course I'm a declamatory poet, I write for the voice, usually mine, or for multiple voices. I'm also more interested in 'resonance' than 'meaning'. And, increasingly, I've started to think about words as music, rather than as 'poetry'

Ralph Hoyte

SALAMI-SLICING THE INTERNAL LANDSCAPE

Ralph Hoyte

THE SALAMI-SLICING INTERNAL LANDSCAPE

Ralph Hoyte

SALAMI-SLICING THE INTERNAL LANDSCAPE
or: from Salcombe to Dartmouth on the SW Coastpath
a walk-poem
by Ralph Hoyte

(EXTRACT)

green sea witch you sing hill to rock. rock to pebble.
pebble to sand. sand to sea. sand to ministry of roads
and transport Salcombe by-pass scheme. they all sing
HERE I AM! the hills the gorse the waves the sea all
affirm my solicitude of being. HERE YOU ARE, SEA
WITCH! Ah me, she's not deaf. shouting is all very
well, but you really want your beautifulness to be as
transparent as a rabbit's burrow on a dark night in a
thunderstorm on Start Point with no crosses Cornish
or otherwise in the way and certainly no skedaddling
down to Bronze Age boats laden with palstave axes
fine tanged swordblades with incised lines at Gara
Rock
[STOP]
um. there's a pointy-eared mongrel cur over thataway
near Beesands called 'Lucky' (1994). talking of fishing
they're arched to the pelargonia. I mean pelargoniums
- red flower things. life… lives off life. there is no way
round it. none. an apple, which if it tastes of anything,
tastes of New Zealand mush ice-cream dropped at
Kingsbridge grit that pigeon looks interested in my
dead pig sandwich you know that silence that hangs
on boughs mesmerised by seadrift on slopes of
bracken above Lannacombe Beach? no. whatever I
say, she says no, don't you? yes. told you so. you
don't know that silence is not necessarily silent, don't
you? the wind is most silent when it blows the hardest,
yet even a bossy-boots of a little girl is louder than the
loudest volcano. maybe Chopin knows. you've got a
point there. a blunt one, but a point. don't … eat me!
ah there's a nibble, most nibblesome, just nibble me
back and I'll… back off! there's miles to go yet to
Dartmouth. miles

A FOLLOWING PAGE

Alicia Grace

A Following Page

Alicia Grace

a following page

a poetic pageant
across the South Hams

celebrating Ivybridge mobile library service

In Service and Desire:
Reading and Writing the Unceremonious Pageantry of a Mobile Library in the South Hams

Attending to hidden, lesser-touched, minoritised & marginalised pockets of place & people is at the heart of my artistic manifesto. When Wordquest first approached me to create a project, they asked for work in the vein of this manifesto for a project that would uncover something or somewhere in Devon not readily celebrated by traditional tropes of literature about place. Uncovering Devon's social ecologies through reading, writing and performance has been the focus of my arts practice for several years, so the invite was fitting.

2012 has been an inescapably ceremonious year, with many a chance to encounter processions of boats, bikes, torches, all being waved on by streams of on-lookers and reams of bunting. In contrast to this ceremonialism, 2012 has also been a year of drastic cuts to the welfare state, which have left the arts sector and library services alike, feeling bruised. The idea of creating a project, in the spirit of Jubilant & Olympiad times against a backdrop of unprecedented changes to the welfare state was a challenge. I wanted to harness the opportunity to write my way into these themes and create a quest which engaged with the conflicting spirits of the time. The processive yet enduring nature of rural mobile library services captured the collision of pageantry and democracy that I was looking for; it also captured my heart and my imagination.

My earliest memory of visiting a library is of boarding the mobile library that parked- up next to the local shops on the council estate where I grew-up. It was on this bus where my undying-love of libraries was ignited. As a teenager my first employment was as a Saturday page (a junior assistant) in a library on a neighbouring estate. Libraries are where I discovered a love of poetry, where I learned about the necessity of a place in which everyone can access the possibilities of knowledge for free; a place from which people could find and compose their own education or entertainment.

The intention behind my Wordquest, *a following page*, was to find myself a role to play within a local mobile library service, to discover the languages lurking within this context, and from this process of engagement, to compose a selection of texts which were relevant in both content and form to the service. For four weeks of *a following page* I hopped on and off routes with the Ivybridge mobile library service, courtesy of one very accommodating librarian, Steve Palmer, and his customers, who welcomed me with curiosity and warmth. Ivybridge mobile library is one of eight mobile library services ran by Devon libraries which visits over 50 stops in parishes across the South Hams district of Devon, on a fortnightly rota. While aboard, I talked, listened, wrote and read. I learned which books were popular with readers and about their lives, drank their homemade elderflower cordial, met their memories of village life and their dogs.

I learned that the romantic literary genre of family saga, so popular with village readers, was some kind of reflection of the places and the people I was visiting. Rather than dismiss the formulaic nature of this writing style (often referred to as 'Aga-saga') I decided to work with it as a central theme of the project. The Norse mythmakers, with whom the literary origin of saga sits, themselves embraced and repeated themes of family and duty as a mode of story telling. Formula based writing is not exclusive to saga, however, examples of literature which work to or follow a procedure can also be found in twelfth century Troubadours of Southern France, the experimental poets of post war America, and many writers since and in-between. Just as the library inexorably repeats a circuit of villages, the sagas it carries engage with writing as ritual repetition, circling in a formula of family, memory, duty, desire and disaster all embedded in rural England – often in Devon itself.

Utilising photocopied pages from saga stories set in Devon I invited mobile library customers to make 'cut-up' poems. The idea behind the process of cut-up poetry is to make explicit the labour and craft involved in creating text, and to acknowledge that all writing is 'borrowed' from the language surrounding us in the everyday. Cut-ups de-romanticise the perceived nature of writing (and the writer), and challenge established norms and forms of literature. Most of all they are an accessible way to play with words, and encourage people to feel their way into language in ways they might not normally do. In a sense the cut-ups made on the library bus offered readers a chance to take the lexicon of saga and re-frame it in their own pattern.

To further the correlation between the processive and repetitive labour of the mobile library and writing, I also attempted to write a poem, in a complex verse form known as the sestina. The sestina, invented by Troubadour Arnaut Daniel, uses a procedure which requires that the same six end words occur in each of the six stanzas, but in a different order according to a fixed pattern. The Troubadours and Trobairitz were early word questers, touring their lyrical poetry to the Provençal courts in the twelfth century. These poets used innovative rhyming or complex patterns within their poems, technical craft being the distinguishing feature of their work. Aside from these technical abilities, the Troubadours were celebrated for their lyrics of free and courtly love, though they also composed songs of debate and songs of service. My sestina for *a following page* entitled *Fortune Lanes* can be read as a service song to Ivybridge mobile library. It can also be read as a love poem. In both content and form *Fortunes Lanes* is a piece which recognises the enduring feat of operating such a service, the accessible pageantry that it plays in the lives of its loyal users, and the cultural life-line which it casts to rural residents who would otherwise be without a place to love and learn from.

Alicia Grace

I would like to give my thanks and acknowledge credit to the following people for their contributions to a *following page*:

Steve Palmer for accommodating the project & me: for his conversation, openness & sense of humour. For sharing his knowledge (& testing mine!) & becoming an unknowing collaborator on the project.

all of the library customers who joined in the spirit of 'cutting-up' & others who entertained us with poetry recitals along the way.

Richard Povall at Aune Head Arts for the invitation and Sarah Cobley at Wordquest for her perseverance.

Shelley Castle for her drawing & photography.

Matthew James & Kate Amphlett, for their dialogue on the sestina.

A. Medlicott & Toby Morgan for attentive support.

daughters.

Hester tilted the frame, looking for herself in the old, faded ~~snaps~~ ~~in Che~~ that how she'd been in that last summer before the war: chin tilted, with an almost heart-breaking look of fearless expectation? Edward, much taller – cheerful and ~~~~ in an open-necked shirt – had his hand on her shoulder. Their cousin and Edward's contemporary, Blaise, must have been behind the camera.

Abruptly she laid the photograph face downwards on the chest. which breaking of the glass had caused some kind of ~~fish lyri~~ rupture in her memory, cracking open the concealing layers of forgetfulness. She was seized by a sudden, formless panic – as if the break presaged bad luck. That was connected with mirrors, not ordinary glass, she told

Fortune Lanes
a sestina for Ivybridge mobile library service
Alicia Grace

This wagon, its body beaten by branches
is hedged with books in rows, tight as ancient lanes.
Through hissing doors villagers board and announce their news, like players in a pageant.
Old hands empty their bags,
then search through stacks, laid with braids of saga.
Behind the counter stands a teller, a seer who scans hands or reads fortune mapped in leaves.

He knows folk through their spines, and the shape of their lives by the veins in their leaves.
For these are the acts of a travelling branch:
remembering, reciting titles of bar-coded saga
shelving routes of fiction in alphabetical lanes
bundling blood & thunder like apples into bags
the pickings of the pageant.

A ritual harvest, this pageant
issuing streams of stories imprinted on leaves
a fortnight's hoard packed in & out of bags,
labelled requests borrowed from other branches
find holt in hydrangea decorated lanes -
the duty & desire of discharging saga

but this bus knows its own saga
of discharge. For like many a tableau of sharp times a pageant
is open to paper cuts - some lanes
have already been erased to leave
readers without the grasp of a branch.
How the hollow priorities of politics make flaccid bags

and those who come from beyond village vistas, with bags
full of fortune, vacate the habit of saga.
A home grown for holiday can fracture branches;
swift visitors need not speak the patient language of pageant
akin with butterflies, who bask on the heat of a bonnet, then leave
and chase in flirtation through lanes.

Waiting is a way of life in these time tabled lanes
and with seasoned rhythm, folk know how to bag
chapters and turn the leaves.
These lives, close knit & sown in saga
are stitched in time to the fabric of pageant -
with borrowed crops they have fed this animate beast of a branch.

Through passages of parish lanes this hard-backed branch ploughs pageant
where words are burrowed into bags and no saga is left unturned,
where a slow and routed rite of reading, leaves players fared well for books.

a page for word-play:

narrow love

implacably. parallel

Porlock direction

compromise, clenched

a page for word-play:

ascertain

firmly. declare?

Patricia, speak,

converging light, circles

a page for word-play:

alliance

tramping this careless drama

waiting will power voice

a page for word-play:

body two,

very lights.

question daughter authorities

The tom-cat

majority

then he's back

in piece

a page for word-play:

a page for word-play:

vigorous

daughter

sack

photograph

body

glimmer

events

Clio

SHORT STORY

Short Story

Foreword

These stories are glimpses of lives, real, imagined or mostly both at once. The lives are linked to one another by place – "this is definitely Devon" as the collaborating writers of *The Literary Festival* concur – and also by the writers' interest in place.

In Gemma Seltzer's *Speak to Strangers*, we watch the Olympic Torch as it passes from hand to hand from our south coast to the north, each bearer or spectator revealing a portion of their history simply through their location on the route and the reasons why they chose to be there. Through the stories found on the *Storytrail*, we travel across moors and forests, through parks and disused buildings, stumbling across elves and fairies, and soaring – remarkably frequently – on the wings of eagles or magical horses. In *The Literary Festival*, we are guided step by step through the grounds of Dartington Hall, eavesdropping on the words and thoughts of picnickers and observing the ways in which the neatly manicured environment interacts with the blithe activities of its inhabitants, both human and animal. And in Roland H. Tuson's moving memoir, *My Exeter*, we peel back eighty years to see the familiar territory of Exeter's river and canal "changed beyond recognition", the air thick with the smoke from steam trains and the water busy with ships, yet still as 'fresh and green' as yesterday.

Each time these stories pause to capture a life in space, they capture it also in time. From the schoolboy taking a daring short cut through the slums of Exeter's West Quarter in 1932, to the Torch Relay spectator snatching a glimpse of the procession before heading off to work in 2012, these everyday happenings are turned into "snapshot moments" by the precise and evocative words of these writers. These stories reveal a human Devon in its layers of time and memory, in its close relationship with the land, the sea and the animal world, and preserve it, in this 'snapshot year' of 2012, for the future.

Clare George

Speak to Strangers: 2012

A column of fire travelling across the UK for 70 consecutive days? Carried by 8,000 different people, along pavements and fields, rivers and mountains? It sounded bizarre and fairly dangerous, but turned into an opportunity for people to take pride in their cities, towns and villages and celebrate the best their community had to offer.

During May 2012, I followed the journey of the Olympic Torch Relay through Devon, from Plymouth to Lynmouth, and wrote twelve stories of a hundred words inspired by the occasion.

The stories aimed not only to reflect the relay itself, but also Devon's distinct geography, history and landscape. I chose to weave a layered narrative by incorporating interviews with many of the torchbearers, texts from regional historical magazines and words from some of the finest local writers including Henry Williamson and Ted Hughes.

I enjoyed watching the crowd as much as the arrival of the torch. In Plymouth, huge numbers swelled onto the Hoe. Teenagers wore Union Jack flags as capes and everyone – everyone - cheered when the torch arrived. Later, in Torquay, elderly ladies had bunting as hairbands. By Exeter Cathedral, entire families were dressed in red, white and blue. Each story was based on moments and conversations shared with these people, and so many others, as the flame passed from hand to hand.

With thanks to the Olympic torchbearers who generously took part in the project, and whose words enriched the stories: Tamara Dixon, Tony Hill, Mark Ormrod, Barbara Snowling, Anna Venn and Serena Waters.

The stories were originally published on a dedicated website: www.speaktostrangers2012.com.

Gemma Seltzer

SPEAK TO STRANGERS

SPEAK TO STRANGERS

#1 Teignmouth

The light lingers on the hill line, where trees are dark, where the fields glow green. By Teignmouth, the weather lifts. You ask me what I read and why I'm here, and I answer with Thomas Hardy and strangers. You are an officer, an advisor, son of an aging father. You are a tightrope walker between two stages of life. Balancing. Scorn for the Jubilee and Olympics charge from you, powerful as a horse. Your childhood on the moors was good. It was good, you say. Good. At Newton Abbot, you and your folded newspapers and your neat spectacles depart.

#2 Plymouth City Centre

Let's say I'm drifting out of a haberdashery shop and perhaps I fall into step with you. Maybe your thoughts are rolling from side to side in your mind, like marbles. It could be that I question whether this is a typical Plymouth Saturday, and that you say it's the Lord Mayor's Show. You might move swiftly; pace as quick as winter nightfall, using your time well. Why don't we agree you have white hair, like candy floss on your head? Let's imagine you never believed you'd look like this. Age, to you, was just the roadside's car-glimpsed tree rot.

#3 Barbican, Plymouth

Eight morris dancers skip along the Barbican, raising sticks, bells and legs in pairs. Jangle, tap, jangle. One performer closes his eyes, dreaming and also leaping, so the moment contains both the jump and the stillness simultaneously. You, meanwhile, watch the scene unfold from your shop doorway, fingers interlaced. In your window display, there are Jubilee bouquets and garlands of red, white and blue. Standing by you, I see your skin is creamy, mascara eyelashes a procession of navy. You are proud of this city, of these people; and the words you speak are blankets to wrap around them all.

#4 The Hoe, Plymouth

Smeaton's Tower is a Cyclops in the distance, with its fixed lightbulb gaze. The city waits for the torch to arrive, urging it to race through neighbouring streets and speed to us. And here you are, a boy with beer and a friend. Here you are, telling us you love our dog, saying he's a gentle one. And now – don't look – here you are offering your lips for licks, your chin and both your cheeks. Your voice repeats, returns, releases, it's a clacker, which you sound until your wrist aches. The evening has arms, and sweeps you into its crevice.

Day 2

#5 Alma Road, Plymouth

Unhelped by any wind, I march along silent streets and an underpass.
You're waiting alone, assured, lilac anorak, blonde bob. I pass you once,
taking the hill in my stride. Then return to share your perfectly selected
position. It's early morning, and the streets are bare. Last night, you were
part of the management, wearing a blazer, passing children balloons.
Today, you're merely a spectator. The sole unquiet thing is the helicopter
overhead, circling through the lace curtain clouds. As the torchbearer
approaches, gold and white, faces are expectant and cameras are poised.
These are the snapshot moments in life.

#6 North Embankment, Dartmouth

I am eyeing up the Queen and Prince Philip when your granddaughter slaps
me with her Union Jack flag, twice. How we laugh, how I inwardly frown.
The royal couple are wearing paper masks. She touches his shoulder with
light fingers and he stretches back in his wheelchair to reciprocate, chuckling
to himself as he poses for another photograph. The sponsors' buses crow:
Hello! Hello on the balconies! Are you all having a good time? Back on our
side of the road, you say you moved from Hackney to Dartmouth, and that
your children glowed, letterboxed, crabbed, because of it.

#7 Babbacome Road, Torquay

On the low stone wall, we swing our legs and discuss the Rotary Club and
the timings of the relay advance party. Later, you click the shutter release,
capturing the sharp smart now of the torchbearer and I, standing smiling.
You hand my camera back and then I lose you in the crowd. I think you had
dark hair. You wore a single gold chain. Your nerves might have been fine, or
they might not have been. You look with pale blue hollow eyes, or soft hazel
ones. You could be a train driver, a mountaineer, or a trapeze artist.

#8 High Street, Exeter

We are edging the car forward and listening to your voice on the radio.
Within the hour, I find you on Exeter High Street. Here, the pavements
are swaying with sunglasses and small children on adult shoulders. Straw
hat and leather jacket, your eyes are searching like the slow sun. You'll be
travelling across the country in a van, with a route that is the labour of
your thirty years. All that space and emptiness ahead. All those country
lanes. May you see the Willow Warbler, scare resident but very local. May
you find Redpoll and Whinchats on Dartmoor, migrant.

Day 3

#9 The Quay, Exeter

It's the earliest start the torch has experienced and Exeter is lining the streets. I count school uniforms and briefcases, listen to a rowing club chant. Quayside I stand, watching the mother flame alighting the golden torch. With a spark, the relay has begun. You and I consider the white tracksuit zipping alongside the water. Your jacket hangs loose, as though reluctant to commit to one specific shape. Into the air, you say, That's that then. I reply, Did you enjoy it? You say, Well, it was all done before I have to get to work, so I can't complain.

#10 North Walk, Barnstaple

Stopping to talk to you is the brightest moment of the day. You're filled with good will, gratefulness, unabashed joy, but you don't know how to express such feelings. Your granddaughter shows me her photographs, but it's you I want to hear from. Talking, you're a river dashing downstream. Gesturing, you're flicking away the stray drips, this excess emotion. Your niece is about to perform on stage, a dance routine rehearsed weekly, for months. The relay was swift and the spectators well behaved, each child sitting neatly on the pavement and waving flags. I wish you'd have screamed; if you'd wanted.

#11 Lee Road, Lynton

Wait, then take a photograph with two torchbearers, you say. But the crowds don't understand. This is their first sighting of a relay runner, so you are tugged and positioned. The torch is slipped from your grip. I notice your grey plait tapers to a fine point. Cameras snap. Your stare is fixed. Not on the road, but somewhere else beyond. You're part of a chain you may never see: you started as a tall brunette, became a teenage boy, turned the corner as a champion fundraiser and ended the race with hair red as flames facing the Somerset border.

#12 Lynmouth Hill, Lynmouth

Framed by two trees: one bursting with leaves, the other twisted and bare, we watch the sun drop behind the sea. You and I eat chips in the company of seagulls. Aiming your food at the birds, you tell me about your day painting window frames. The torch passed and you didn't raise your head: a living to make and there's no time to spare. We speak of the model railway museum, how careful fingers made tiny figures and crafted town buildings smaller than matchboxes. In the background, the handmade 'welcome' banners still hang, the ribbons curl, the flags sway.

Storyboxes containing blank books were placed across Devon for people to discover and add their own creative contribution to the expanding stories.

In keeping with Wordquest Devon's links to the Cultural Olympiad, the Storytrail project used the concept of relay-race running and turned it into a relay-race of literary imagination.

We'd like to thank the following writers for providing the opening sentence for each book: Helen Dunmore, Graham Gammin, Joanne Harris, Marina Lewycka, Hilary Mantel and Deborah Moggach.

With special thanks to artist Charlie Henry for creating Storytrail for Wordquest Devon.

STORYTRAIL

a relay of literary imagination

STORYTRAIL

a relay of literary imagination

Roland's False Teeth

Having lost his false teeth somewhere in the grounds that morning, Roland greeted the woman waiting for him at Dartington Hall with a tight lipped smile.

He thrust his hand out, she ignored and walked past him as if she hadn't seen him. Her coat flapped behind her like the wings of a bat and she sniffed loudly so Roland wouldn't approach her again.

Roland ran his tongue over his gums. It was more than a little off putting, he admitted.

All he had to do, surely, was to retrace his steps. He had his teeth in at breakfast, he had gone up to his room to finish his ablutions and he was sure they had been in place then.

When he got back to his to his room there were muddy paw prints on the carpet, the window was open and in the distance he saw a dog with his teeth in his mouth smiling back at him with a cheeky grin.

So he grabbed nearest cat, jumped on his back and gave chase.

With wings they began to fly high over Dartington Hall, looking at all the beauty in the grounds. Looking high and low for the false teeth.

As Roland began to back track his tracks realised he had dropped them down the toilet when he was pulling the chain after going to the loo.

He went back to his room as quick as he could and found them floating in the toilet bowl, picked them out and boiled them up in some water to clean them, popped them into his mouth and smiled.

His smiled cracked the glass with a terrible crack. His smile grew broader and he knew what he had to do.

Quick as flash, he picked up his pistol, thrust them into his breeches and ran out of his room down the oak staircase and out into the grounds. A flash of lightning lit up the cobbled path and rain whipped his hair across his evil features.

Roland had met a perfectly lovely looking lady with ever such a sweet smile and the sharpest tongue he had come across. Now here he was with a devastating smile of a very different nature.

Once he was twenty, looking at the world inviting him and woman seemed so much nicer.

The circumstances were less than perfect both of them were burdened by luggage and there were remnants of lunch between his teeth.

"Sometimes I can think of nothing but teeth," she said "they become a mono-subject. It's teeth, just teeth rows of them like piano keys."

"All soup tureens," he replied somewhat facetiously.

Haldon Nick

It's odd that I never met him, when for all those year he was living in the house next door.

Suddenly there was a big noise from outside and he went to the door to have a look, but nothing was there, I watched him step outside.

He was fat and hairy with teeth as sharp as a saw. He was very intriguing to watch.

For a moment I was very scared but then I decided to say hello.

The estranged fellow's name was Doctor Nick.

He had been tracking elves through Haldon Forest his whole life with little success, and so the question is why was he doing such a crazy thing?

He was being blackmailed by the King of Haldon Forest, who was a very bad man, who wanted it all for himself, except of course for his beautiful wife, the only person or thing that he truly wanted! But she was hiding deep, deep in Haldon woods.

So the King had ordered Doctor Nick to search for her, for she was in fact an elf, the most beautiful one of all.

Elves are extremely small and live up in the trees in the forest, as this is an excellent place to see all the people visiting and play tricks on them.

One elf placed a rock on the road and caused a crash.

But as the elf was magic, no one was injured.

But the poor elf lost a toe, his shoes no longer fitted him and his eyeball fell out.

Obviously the elf was magic and so the toe grew back. Unfortunately a giant half chicken, half squirrel (common in the forest) ate the rouge eyeball. Luckily the other was ok, so he could still keep an eye out for the lost Queen.

The Queen however, was looking after her baby daughter and didn't know the elves were still looking for her. They looked everywhere, high and low, near and far, there and back again.

One bright day the King saw his Queen and baby daughter in a shaft of sunlight. They were reunited over a roast wild pig, lived happily ever after and the King was nice now he was happy!

I have been attacked by the gulls several times, so now I always climb the fixed ladder to the roof under the shelter of my grandfather's golf umbrella.

Having reached the roof and caught the offending gull with a bait of bacon butties, I was surprised to find the gull now attached itself to me, all aggression gone, to be replaced by what could be called affection, yellow eyes fixed on my every move, edging closer when I made to move away. On closer inspection it was a beautiful white winged Pegasus representing a portal to my imagination, helping me to understand that there is a thin veil between reality and my dreams.

As the rain paved down, coating the white wings with pearls of water, I wondered what a Pegasus eats. Getting wetter and wetter the Pegasus opened his wings to their glorious fullness. Someone whispered...

"Everyone knows the Pegasus eats golden breadfruit from the end of the rainbow."

The thing about eating gold breadfruit from the end of the rainbow is that it gives them magical powers and enables them to fulfil dreams – but in order to release the power, you first have to catch the Pegasus, so I did.

And as I sat astride the Pegasus looking down on trees of Dartington to the retracted rainbow I realised

My sister is very annoying

"Sisters!" said Pegasus and "Families!" and he sighed and his eyes took on a distant look. "But not now," he said firmly and began to hear a snuffling noise just behind him – he turned but couldn't find the source of the noise, until suddenly something he thought was a rock moved... "Hello there," said the horse, "I'm dreaming of galloping across the open moorland to a distant tor where the views stretch out across the lowland fields to the sea beyond."

I then dived into the fast flowing waterfall, and the sound became beautiful music... a lightless filled my heart and I swam downstream with the flow, flipping onto my back I saw a spec in the sky which, as it flew closer, revealed itself to be a Pegasus with a boy clinging to its neck.

Reaching up I took hold of its feet and was lifted from the water; however, a large duck took hold of my toe, a moorhen dangled from the duck's foot and a tiny frog leapt up and clung on to the moorhen. We flew off like a kite ribbon.

I had always wanted to fly, a devotee of Jonathan Livingston seagull, no longer afraid the gulls were a threat, just fellow travellers along with Pegasus and his followers, that boy was me!

After all this I felt quite hungry, I prepared a plate of fresh figs (they were just ripe in my garden) black olives, Dutch cheese and parsley. The birds all flew off. They were, after all, birds. I wanted to share the meal with someone, and I realised I had never really spoken to my next door neighbour, a small old man with a whiskery moustache, dressed in tweed and smelling of parchment and tobacco. I knocked on his door, it swung open immediately.

He turned out to be a veteran from the Second World War and had many fascinating tales to tell about his life in the navy and the many strange creatures he had encountered in his travels, one of which was Pegasus.

The war veteran turned out to be a close friend of my grandfather. It was he who explained to me why my grandfather's umbrella had magical powers.

The most important thing, he explained, was to understand how the magic golf umbrella could be used to the very best of advantages. Apparently its most powerful attribute was the umbrella's ability to be a shelter for the little people playing games, small animals in a rainstorm and to listen to secrets.

Pegasus took flight on the jet stream and turned it north into the sunlight landscape of Devon. It was a warm July evening, with moisture dangling like jewels on a spider's web. All was still, the squirrels had stopped for the evening and no one was about, and yet one somehow had the strongest sensation that something was about to happen.

A man sitting on a bench looked up at the boy on the horse in the sky, but all he saw was wind – dragged clouds, which slowly transformed into the shape of a recumbent mermaid.

The rainbow touched the grass but as the children excitedly approached, it sped across the trees over a hill and out to sea.

Only Pegasus can catch the rainbow and he was still circling overhead tantalisingly close but just out of reach.

As I sat pondering on this seat a little worm peeped out at me.

"Is it safe for me to come and see? I know the black bird has his eyes on me." "His singing has stopped. He may have gone," I replied. "Oh," said the worm." "I had to come – I nearly died when rain first came, all night and day I thought I would be swept away."

But just as we were pondering how best to help the worm a retired gardener called Rosemary appeared wearing enormous wellington boots. "Crawl inside," she said "there's plenty of room for you to hide amongst my toes. I will take you with me wherever I go and you can travel the world and if I ever see Pegasus again I will ask him to take you on board."

I popped 'Hedwig' into my handbag, kicked Mercury into touch and threw Pegasus aloft where it flipped open and transformed again into the winged horse. Climbing onto its broad back, I cast a swift glance back at the booted worm and then soared back into the rain soaked hills.

I headed east high over the hills towards the Pyrenees and eventually descended into a strange sculptural garden by the Mediterranean where I met Salvador Dali riding his newly fashioned rocking horse. He asked me to join him where we rocked together energetically with such combined power we took off over the sea.

Do you think if we wish hard Pegasus will come back?

We closed our eyes and let our minds wander to the happy moments we shared with our feathered friend, Pegasus. All of a sudden we heard something approaching us, sure enough when I opened my eyes Pegasus had returned. I ran over and hugged him tightly, so ecstatic that he was back I whispered,

"Thank god you're back, quick get me out of here." But just as quickly as he had appeared Pegasus disappeared again.

We carried on and on and on looking for our friend. We sat on a bench to rest – it was so peaceful and quiet we drank, ate and dozed, thinking.... wondering if we'd been left behind, where were they, did they want to see us again, what to do next?

Miraculously, as we stood by the letterbox there was a familiar whinny and Pegasus was back! We jumped on his back and flew up into the cloudy sky. We knew he wouldn't leave us again and that he would protect us on our journey to …

"There used to be six," she said, "but now there is only one left."

Ben turned to Holly and said, "Did you eat one?"

"No, I didn't," said Holly. "Those things are disgusting."

"Well you know what's in them, right?"

"Exactly. And you know what that does to you?"

"Enlightenment."

"But one of them turned up," said Sammy, "it was underneath a bush."

"Do you think it's a fairie child or left by some poor village girl who knew not which way to turn?" he pondered.

Fred came along and said,

"Once I was here but now am gone, but I shall return it won't be long."

At the door of the water mill stood a tall man with a 3 cornered hat.

"My name is Digger Ben," said the tall man.

"I am just going to the water mill. I love water mills and adventures."

The water mill was dark against the evening sky and owls were calling forlornly from across the river. Holly, Ben and Sam exchanged nervous glances then straightened their shoulders and marched up to the door. The mill wheel was still creaking round. Deep inside the mill they could just make out the gurning of metal.

"Shall we knock?" Ben suggested.

A moment later a window opened with a groan and a face peered over the window sill.

"Take the path by the underground stream and find where the water goes."

So they set off down towards the meadow not knowing they were being followed, watched by a shadowy figure just out of sight.

Deciding to ignore the figure as their mum had told them, they joined voices in perfect harmony and sang 'Irene Goodnight'.

The shadowy figure appeared to stop for a moment, turned and then disappeared behind a tree.

Sam was becoming restless with domesticity, despite its obvious attractions.

He long to swap the hum-drum for the 'am-dram' or the mundane in order to profane!

He stepped out into daybreak, early one cold morning and looked calmly at the view before him.

He walked off into the trees when suddenly a thought occurred to him. What if I didn't walk into the trees? What if I did the exact opposite of what is expected of me?

As he walked the opposite direction he could see two women ahead. He called to them to ask,

"Where are you going and can I come with you?"

The taller of the two turned to regard the speaker, but to her abject alarm her notorious faulty knee buckled under the sudden pivot, rendering her helpless with a face caked in dirt.

They then skip through the meadows into the sunset and the portal to another dimension

where one could again see five trees, which, overnight, had raised themselves up.

"I could swear," said she, "I stand in the centre, whisper the dreams of my heart."

"I wonder if those words will be heard?"

Giant clouds gathered overhead, large raindrops began to fall.

All of a sudden, the animals far and wide broke into a cacophony that pierced the rain-drenched hills.

She just stood there, staring, and she wept.

Suddenly, a fox jumped out, startled by what he saw, he growled then ran towards a mist which quickly enveloped him.

"I'm not coming here again," she said, "it gives me the shivers." But suspected she probably would, sooner or later.

She eventually came back after 2 hours and spoke to her little friend.

As they stood there talking, a voice called out: "Do not turn around, do not turn your head. I am standing behind you but you must not see me. Walk on."

Suddenly a bird whooped and flew out of the trees just over their heads. A huge silence fell.

Why did that thing have to happen? Life had been ok – not perfect but ok. I'd given everything. Then this! Why did this thing happen?

I was confused and I left sad, but feeling sad felt good about feeling sad, but suddenly had the inspirational moment and thought

spring follows winter.

I remember evacuation September 1st 1939. Long trip to where we did not know. Lemonade and a bar of chocolate where we arrived at near Tewksbury. Everyone came to point at a child they wanted but nobody wanted three of us so they all left us standing there. We eventually were left in a stable in a yard. It was the coldest of winters. Not wanting to be half starved. Not forgotten. But now a very happy old lady of 80 years young.

Sometimes the promise of spring is better that the actuality of a summer that is not a summer, the actuality of a holiday that does not fulfil its promise. Let's return to the thing that happened and let the story grow.

The light whose smiles kindles the universe, that beauty in which all things work and move.

That calm infusion of knowing a peaceful aura flowing, overflowing into a meditating mind of placidity.

And then I saw a beautiful sight of a colourful man, much larger than life, with a flower and a feather tucked behind his ear and an eagle with wings outstretched clutched to his chest.

He did not see me, he was looking beyond me to the mountain range tipped with snow. The eagle flapped its wings as if yearning to leave.

To leave or to arrive or the enigma of arrival spring to mind… and who cares about a confused eagle anyway.

You must not disturb the stillness of the sea but float about it until you reach shore and mountain and peace.

I float above the sea's rippling surface and feel the compulsion to immerse myself in the body and spirit within it.

Slowly I sink beneath the surface, the water enveloping me like a cool, welcome shroud.

A dream! It was a dream! It can't have been: it felt so real, so awful, so intense! Back to reality, another Monday morning, kids to get off to school, cold, grey drizzle outside, ow, when will it change?

It had to happen because to feel the real power of the sun you have to feel the cold and rain too.

Mind equipped

With the rewind button

Want to be at peace with myself

A thought and a prayer.

As ever, the story had taken on a life of its own, as voices other than mine flooded onto the page through my pen. I was at a loss how to control the chaos – how to weave a pattern that others could follow, how to make the tale tell itself with clarity.

Yet chaos is abhorred by some and chaos preferred by others. Out of chaos comes clarity. The revelation descended in me like a clap of thunder and suddenly I KNEW why it happened! It was to find a box in the dark to open it and write our story.

We all live out our story together, the same, shared as one, united in the tale with our distinct voices.

It is tranquil here in this Japanese garden.

At twilight, the shadows fall

Memories come back

Coal fires, kindling wood

The blinds drawn

Autumn hurries on.

We throw a pebble in the pond. Its ripples, moving outward, a Big Bang endlessly echoing the shape of the primal splash. And at some point all of our patterns merge.

Tip tap tip tap falls the rain fills the river, and the lane.

What primal energy fired the spins : and yet every particle on earth is made of light – from whence comes the light in the matter?

"Does it even matter?" replied Magda. "It's all getting a bit heavy for me, so let's just press on. Shall we?"

Some people look for beautiful places, others make them.

I wish I knew what I wanted.

Let me start today with a new life please.

Until we really feel compelled to share and feel only happiness doing so, we always will be searching, searching. We have it all and yet we feel we have nothing. Love yourself, nature, family, everything. We are all made up of the same atoms, we are all unique and equal.

The end.

The end? But how can that be? The end follows the beginning. Rhymes and riddles, there is after all only one! Or, the bottom end – without it we wouldn't know where to sit.

We sit where we are placed. By whom? When? Why? We try to find the answers – I sit here in this beautiful Japanese garden. I love the feeling. This is where I come to rest and find myself. To take me away from pain and to listen and watch the beautiful robin come up to me.

He is here to tell me who to trust. Have light and peace. I am what I am!

Roll up! Roll up!
YOUR WORDS WIN PRIZES

HOW TO PLAY

1. Think of a fact, a bit of trivia, a personal experience relating to Devon writers, writing and the Devon landscape

2. Tell it to the Lovely Lady at the Wordquest Tombola stall and in exchange you can...

3. SPIN the tombola drum and WIN something WORDY!

THE PRIZES are an excellent range of literary 'knick-knacks' that have been donated by contemporary writers with a Devon connection.
IF YOU ARE REALLY LUCKY – you could WIN a creative writing task to be done BY YOU in Dartington Hall Gardens. Each task has been specially made for the event by poets, playwrights, artists and authors – or by the Lovely Lady herself.

WHAT ARE YOU WAITING FOR?
HAVE A GO AND WIN A WONDERFUL WORDFUL PRIZE!

The Literary Festival was written during one glorious summer's day at the Ways With Words Festival in Dartington Hall Courtyard by the following adults, children and published authors: Dara Browne, Matt Crick, Margaret Edmonds, Sally Hackney, Molly, Cat Radford, Mary Twist and ANON. It was developed from writing tasks donated by Ginny Baily, Jane Borodale, Sean Borodale, Tania Haberland, John Hall, Natalie McGrath, Shiona Morton, Simon Persighetti, Liv Torc and Caroline Wilson. It was artfully edited (with some additional connecting words) by the Lovely Lady.

Wordquest Tombola was developed and hosted by Paula Lovely Lady Crutchlow. With thanks to all the authors who donated the lovely prizes.

More wonderful Wordquest Tombola writings can be watched online at:
http://www.auneheadarts.net/site/projects/wordquest/wordpress/?page_id=306

THE LITERARY FESTIVAL

a collaborative writing experiment
Ways With Words, Dartington

The Literary Festival

a collaborative writing experiment
Ways With Words, Dartington

Walk eight steps from tarmac onto cobblestones. Sign says Welcome. Walk thirty three steps passing no picnics and ball games and don't tie your bike here. Enter the stone archway. On the right see the noticeboard with map of the gardens. The pile of free newspapers. Hear gentle murmurs and the sound of low heels on stone flags. Sandwich board sign says The Telegraph Ways With Words Festival of Ideas with the daily programme of speakers.

Look up. Move out into the courtyard. See green yellow red blue wooden deckchairs scattered across the closely mown lawn. See the Manor 'continuously occupied for well over a thousand years'. Turn left and circle around the edge. Past the white marquees, the mobile book shop, the well dressed and softly spoken. Hear birdsong and what could be a green woodpecker – the perfect mix of nature and culture. Hear the whispering of broadsheets. See the queue slowly building for the next event. Walk past the grand entrance and do not go in. Further 36 steps pass the low stone wall next to the White Hart Inn. Walk alongside the tall yew hedge and look out towards the thatched summer house. At the end of the hedge. Pause.

Coffee wafts, intrudes, shakes the peace, disturbs the gentleness of all around; chinks of china. This is definitely Devon. They rattle the empty cups and saucers in a rich, cream tea way down here before they're plunged into the soapy suds to be recycled for the next customer. Rucksacked men and women with spotty hats bring poly bags full of books to the cafe.

He: We'll just have time for a cup of tea.

She: And cake. It isn't tea without a piece of chocolate
cake – and it's got beetroot in it.

He: That doesn't make it healthy. It's a myth.

She: I don't care what you think. As far as I'm concerned,
it's one of my five a day and I'm going to enjoy it!

He has very neatly crossed legs, bit too neat. Bright turquoise socks and a politically correct canvas bag. Engrossed in a crossword, eyelids flickering, mouth puffing like a fish. Ragged beard seems completely separate from his very neatly trimmed moustache. The large, wide mouth – clear despite the moustache and always partly open. He sups his drink then throws his head right back to drain the last drop. Tight grip of his hands on pen.

Silence.

Her eyes narrow squinting at something far away across the lawn. She brings the straw to her lips and her mouth grows small, the lips closing tightly, the straw held at the side of her mouth as though she were smoking a pipe. With each sip her head dips forwards, a slow nodding motion. Between sips she cups the plastic beaker in both hands cradling it as though it were something precious and fragile.

She knows that words have many meanings and colour makes people feel different. That everyone feels fear, gets nervous and covers it up, some more than others. She knows that manners cost nothing and that when you stop talking you hear so much more. Time. I feel like I'm running out of time. Always. But being outside makes me feel good. It's good for my soul, makes me calm, connected, energised.

Her gaze draws back from the lawn, and falls upon the little girl sitting across the table. She pauses, her thumb and forefinger twisting the top of the straw. "Are you having a lovely holiday?" She says. Her voice as smooth and kind as the banana milk shake in her hand.

Withdraw and move on. Fifty one steps. Pass the wooden tables with the square canvas umbrellas and the tables with the joined together bench seats. Feet on stone flags. Scrape of knives on plates. Pass another yew hedge. Sign says 'Do not climb though these hedges or allow children inside'. Cross the lawn. Pass the old cedar trees. Sign says 'If you climb on my branches the gardeners will defend me'. Turn right. See Little Bronze Donkey. In your 76 years how many generations have you had on your back? Walk 162 steps past low shrubs and a low stone wall up a gentle incline. Walk up 6 steps from gravel onto stone flags. Look right. Pause. Through a wrought iron gate, through a twisting of clematis. See the Manor 'continuously occupied for well over a thousand years'.

Damp soil sweet musty damp bottoms   sprouting new   remembers footsteps   caught dew   holds life and death, and witness to everything in between.

Walk down 7 steps towards the Sunny Border. Sign says 'Do not climb on the grass banks'. Walk twenty steps. Pause. See the Green Oasis of yew Trees called The Twelve Apostles. In the distance Henrietta Moore lies surveying her terrain. She sees a burnt tree trunk. It's painted black to stop it rotting. She wishes the whole world could be painted to stop it rotting.

Walk approximately 80 steps to the end of the Sunny Border. Turn left and follow the sound of running water.

Sign says Willi Soukup Swan Fountain. Three brothers and their younger sister dip their hands into the cold water sorting through the coins to find foreign treasures. Their mother quizzes them on the subject of a fairytale barely remembered in which a spell is cast that turns the people into swans for 900 years, until the ringing of a magic bell wakes them from their sleeping existence.

She can't help but imagine her own children at the same age. Seeing this future through the misty lens of memory. Certainly before their appearance she would not experience the same kind of nostalgia for a life not yet lived, but so close around the corner. She would neither have said that she'd previously sleepwalked through life, not for a second. But on her arrival her new bundle of joy somehow switched a magic switch, rang a magic bell that woke her to a life previously hidden from view. Willi Soukop said: "My life was never planned, it just happened. "Her life was never planned, not even before them and their lives were never planned either; they just wanted to be here.

Pause. Look out into the distance. Look over the three flights of stairs leading into the Tilt Yard. Look between the banks of steep green terraces and the carefully laid pathways. Over the wild flower meadow to the middle distance of rural idyll. To the green patchwork and the small white cottages on the horizon. This is definitely Devon. Sign says 'Watch your step'. Count 1, 2, 3, 4, etc. on every left foot. Every 100, hold a finger in until 1,000. 1,700 steps to the bridge. 2,300 steps to the sea. But no matter how many steps I take, I never reach my love. Coffee wafts, intrudes, shakes the peace, disturbs the gentleness of all around; bangs in the head. Chinks of china. After all 10 fingers turn left or right and return to the festival. Or stray further into counting land. Without looking back.

Wordquest Devon worked in collaboration with Riptide Journal to produce a volume of short stories and memoirs, which represent the diversity of the county. My Exeter – Canal & River by Roland H. Tuson is one of 15 stories reflecting Devon past, present and future.

MY EXETER-
CANAL & RIVER

Roland H. Tuson

My Exeter- Canal & River

Roland H. Tuson

There is very little that remains of the Exeter I knew as a boy eighty years ago. The Exeter that existed then, in particular that area in which I spent my boyhood days, the canal and river, has today changed beyond recognition.

It was almost a year following my birth in December 1923 that I was brought by my parents from my birthplace in Bournemouth and left in the care of an elderly lady known locally as Nurse West. From then, I lived with and was brought up by this lady. I remained with her until I was thirteen, during which time there were occasional visits by my parents who had settled and found more regular employment in Sidmouth. Mrs West lived in a very small terrace house, 2 Tisards Cottages, on the banks of the canal just a few yards from a pub: 'The Welcome Inn', which still stands there today, though the row of small houses is long gone. The house consisted of one small room with a coal fire and oven, and the front door opened directly into this room. Beyond, through an opening, there was a tiny room no bigger than a cupboard. On the rough earthen floor stood a gas cooker, and from here a narrow steep staircase went up to the two bedrooms. Under the stairs, there was the coal hole.

The only lighting was given by two gas lamps over the fireplace in the front room and one over the gas cooker. There were no lights in the upstairs rooms. Water had to be carried in from an adjoining communal wash-house in which stood three toilets – one for each of the first three houses in the terrace. These toilets were very primitive, each consisting of a rough wooden compartment with a wooden seat containing the usual aperture. Underneath there was a bucket which a man came and emptied weekly, by which time there was no shortage of flies.

As I grew and came to be more aware of my surroundings, I understood just how very poor Nurse West was and what a day to day struggle life was for her. Her only income was her weekly old age pension, a brown ten shilling note – just 50p in today's currency – and perhaps a few shillings whenever my father came to see us, but that was not often. She had a reputation among the local people as a nurse. She would mix medicines, visit the sick and give advice to the family on how to care for the patient, who nearly always recovered. She never made any charge but those who were working would always give whatever they could afford. In spite of her poverty, I cannot ever recall a single day when I went hungry. My clothes were shabby, patched and repaired but always respectable.

From a young age I addressed Nurse West as Grandma even though my father said she was not my real Grandma (he did not tell me who my real grandma was). At the end of a week she would send me up to a small shop in West Street to buy a farthing packet of tea, enough to make just one pot. Many years later, just before he died, my father told me that he had never known his father or mother and that Nurse West had brought him up.

My memories of my schooling are very hazy. At age five I was sent to St Nicholas that was then situated in Mint Lane at the top of Fore Street hill. The school was run and staffed by the nuns from the nearby Convent. My only clear memory is how very strict and ready to use the cane with a heavy hand they were, however, I was never a victim of these extreme punishments.

Later, when I was older I moved into the Mint Methodist School for boys, also in Mint Lane. I remember little of the lessons or the teachers, but geography and reading were my favourites. It is strange but I never remember being taught to read, but read I did from a very early age. My journey to school took me across the river on the ferry, up Coombe Street and then South Street. There was a short-cut through the West Quarter, which was where the very poorest people of the city lived in the most crowded and unsanitary conditions. I was warned that if I went through it I would catch some terrible disease or be robbed of the little I had. Nevertheless, as a young child I did just the opposite of what I was told and often cut through this forbidden territory. I never came to any harm.

Between the ages of six and twelve the canal, and the wonderful sweep of fields, orchards and farmlands through which the river flowed to the sea, provided one huge adventure playground for me and my friends to explore. We let our imaginations take us where they would. One day we were cowboys fighting the redskins, another we were explorers looking for lost cities in the jungle and, when a ship came up the canal, we became pirates ready to board her and seize the treasure. Sometimes, as a ship was passing through Double Locks, we would call to the master and ask if we might come aboard. On the very rare occasions that we were waved aboard, we pretended we had taken the ship, but we never did manage to get the crew to walk the plank. We had, in any case, to jump ashore as the ship went through the next swing bridge. We roamed far and wide on those long warm summer days in perfect freedom. There was never any need for anyone to worry about us.

The Gregory family, who ran the ferry, also had a floating pontoon at Shooting Marsh Stile from which there was a large selection of boats for hire. These boats were designed mainly for two people. They had a passenger seat at the stern with a backrest and armrests either side for the lady. The passenger (the lady) was supposed to steer the boat by pulling on one of two cords that moved the rudder.

In the long, warm evenings of summer, these boats became a small source of income for us. The young men and their ladies would flock down to the river to hire a boat and row down to The Double Locks. On the return journey, after having a drink or two, many would pull into the canal bank and wander off into the fields to continue their courting. We would walk slowly along the tow path looking for abandoned boats. The halfpenny reward was very quickly spent in the nearest sweet shop on Haven Road.

In Cotfield Street, situated a few yards further down the canal from our house, there was another sweet shop, Mrs Warren's, which was in the front room of her house. We boys sometimes spent our halfpennies there but it was always a nervous experience. She regarded us with a suspicious eye and was careful to see our money first for which we were given the exact weight of confectionary and then shooed out. It wasn't so much her manner that made us nervous, but her appearance. Almost the whole of one side of her face was terribly disfigured with a vivid red-wine birthmark. Looking back I can only wonder at the courage with which she went through her life, to open a shop and face the public every day – no wonder she was grumpy with a bunch of young boys.

At that period in time (1925-1935) Exeter was still a busy maritime port and the ships from far and near brought cargo of timber, oil, coal and wines. Ships from across the channel brought the French Onion boys. Just as soon as they got ashore off they went on their bicycles festooned with onions selling from door to door.

Many of the ships were sailing ships with only a small engine as a standby. In the canal, they had to be towed by two large powerful shire horses who were housed in a stable built alongside 'The Welcome Inn'. These stables were knocked down long ago to make room for cars to park, but the back wall may still be seen.

Steam driven ships were kept to a strict speed limit to avoid creating a wash which would damage the banks of the canal. These coastal steamships of 'The Everard Shipping Company' brought coal from Blyth in Northumberland for the Exeter Gaslight & Coke Company. The Ardasity and the Alacrity berthed just inside the Basin dock and discharged their cargo into railway wagons where a small tank engine (much like Thomas the Tank Engine) then took them into the gas works.

The engine driver was a Mr Reginald Hamilton. He lived in a brick built house, one of a terrace owned by the gas company on the canal banks at the end of Cotfield Street. He always carried a handful of sweets in his pockets to give to children when he passed them at play. Mr Hamilton, on a few occasions, while he waited for the trucks to be filled, let me climb onto the engine footplate and showed me how the controls were used and how it worked. Both he and his wife knew my father and mother before I was born and when my parents came to see me, they always went to visit the Hamiltons. They had five daughters: the eldest, Vera, married the cook from one of the coal ships, Charles Hodges, who took her back to his home in London. The remaining four daughters starting with the eldest were Doreen, Phyllis, Beryl and the youngest Eileen. Of these, it is Phyllis I now turn to. When my grandma became too frail to care for me (I was then almost 13 years of age), it was Phyllis who came to help. She chopped wood, fetched coal and kept a fire going. She brought hot soup and other food that her mother had prepared. Phyllis was 15 and had also to go to work to help bring a little money for her family. It was many long years before I was to learn of the debt Phyllis and her family owed to my grandma.

There was one other motor ship that was a regular vessel. She was 'The Ben Johnson', the oil tanker of the Shell Oil Company. She always berthed at the far end of the basin and discharged the oil through large pipes to the storage tanks in the nearby depot.

Depending on their cargos, other ships would enter the river and sail up to berth at the quay, where was situated the Customs House with the Bonded Warehouse nearby. There were also many other warehouses along the quay and in Commercial Road.

Across the river from the quay and opposite the Shilhay, there was a large piece of rough waste ground sandwiched between the river and Haven Road. Here, two or three times a year, the travelling fun fair of Anderson & Rowland would be set up. We boys had no money, but we managed to enjoy ourselves nevertheless. There would be three or four huge traction engines standing along the Haven Road, all spotlessly clean, thundering away to supply the power for all the lights, roundabouts and side shows. Amongst these was the BOXING tent. Before it opened, the barker would parade several muscular men on a raised platform and invite challengers from the watching crowd. Should the volunteer survive and still be on his feet at the end of three rounds, he would win a sum of money. There were always plenty of men willing to try their luck, but most went away empty handed. We boys would find a place at the back of the tent where the canvas was a bit slack and when there was a lot of excitement and shouting from inside, we would quickly crawl under. Sometimes if we were seen by one of the men in the audience they would pull us in and put us forward so we could see better. We saw many fights this way but there was one in particular I well remember. It was the time a local heavy weight champion stepped into the ring. The result was a foregone conclusion even though the barker, who was also the referee, tried to declare it an unfair fight. When he saw that the crowd was ready to start a free for all, the prize money was handed over, the victor thanked the audience and went on his way.

On the other side of the river was a piece of land that we now call The Shilhay, which was an island, separated from the main river by a small creek. This creek was very dark and creepy, hemmed in on one side by tall stacks of wood, the property of the timber merchants Gabrial, Wade & English, and on the other by the backs of warehouses. It was also, as I discovered when I went exploring there with a friend, a breeding ground for rats.

Situated on Haven Road not far from the Basin stood a large imposing building from which as you passed you heard a soft humming, this was Exeter's Electricity Power Station. We had tried many times to see inside but were always chased away by one of the workers. One evening just as it was getting dark I was on my way home, as all seemed quiet I walked quickly up the steps to the main doors which were still open, as there was no one about I gently opened the inner door and looked in. I was amazed, it was one huge long and high hall, the walls were covered with shining tiles and everything was spotlessly clean even the handrails and floors. Down the centre were the giant dynamos giving out that gentle humming we had heard and wondered about. To me it was just like something out of a science fiction magazine. Somebody must have spotted me and shouted, I was off like a rocket and got home in record time but I had at last seen the inside of the power station.

Next to the power station and separated by the railway track that ran from the Basin docks was the large sawmill of Claridges. To these I often would see large tree trunks on long pole wagons drawn by teams of two or four shire horses moving slowly along Haven Road on their way to the saw mill. There the tree trunks were cut into planks or square lengths of various sizes. Adjoining the saw mills was the gas works from which the railway track emerged and ran down to the coal ships.

During the day from early morning until evening this whole area was alive with the sound and bustle of men going about their widely different tasks together with the hum and noise of wagons mixing with machinery of all kinds – it was the beating heart of an old and proud city.

The land opposite my grandma's cottage that divides the canal and river must at some time have been a market garden but had long ago been abandoned and just allowed to grow wild. However, the rows of fruit bushes although overgrown by long grass still bore fruit in abundance. We would cram bowls with redcurrants, raspberries & blackcurrants which we then took home to be made into jellies and jam. We also explored along the river bank and using thin string and bent pins tried fishing, but we never even had a nibble. In summer we could walk across Trew's Weir for the river only trickled over the top of the dam. In winter when the river was in full flow it was a raging torrent. Trew's Weir served two purposes. First it held the river back and maintained the level of water in the canal which it fed through lock gates. It also, via a small leat on the far side, fed the nearby Trew's Mill to power its machinery.

One day we discovered an old boat, it had been pulled out of the water and left. It must have been there a long time for it was overgrown with grass and weeds. In the bottom there was a loose and broken plank which we supposed was why it had been abandoned. This we decided would be our pirate ship and set to work. First we obtained an old orange box. Someone got some nails and borrowed a hammer from his dad. Using wood from the orange box we covered the hole and supported the loose plank. Then we launched our ship – she seemed sea worthy so we climbed aboard and hoisted The Jolly Roger. As soon as we did she filled with water and sank. Fortunately as we were still at the river bank we were able to wade ashore. So we left our ship to the mercy of the river and trudged homeward wondering what excuse we could give for our wet clothes.

There was one day of the year when the river became a great attraction for everyone that was the annual Regatta Day. This day held in summer was a day of sport and fun both on and off the water. On the water there would be numerous boats of all sizes all decorated with flags and bunting; it was a carnival on water. There was also more serious boat racing as rowing clubs and colleges competed in their long racing narrow boats. Along the river banks stood various side shows and stalls. One always very popular attraction was the Greasy Pole contest. This contest consisted of a thick pole, much like a telegraph pole, projecting out over the river. The pole would be smooth and coated with a thick layer of grease to make it even more difficult to get a grip. Two contestants would sit facing each other and using something soft like a stuffed pillowcase try to knock each other off into the river.

There was one part of the river that was not usually used by us as it was mainly a business and small industry area. This was upstream of the Exe Bridge. From the bridge to St David's Railway Station running along parallel with the river is Bonhay Road. Starting at the bridge on land lying between the road and river lay the cattle market, next came various buildings possibly all connected with the market and farming, then came a large mill that manufactured a wide variety of paper, just above this mill there was another weir, this allowed water to run down a leat and provide power to operate the mill. Further up the river there was a section marked out with floating tree trunks where bathing was permitted and was the reason we strayed so far from our usual territory. Access was via a small iron gate situated close to the railway viaduct and down a path to a large iron clad shed in which you could change. Last summer I took a walk along the Bonhay Road, the little gate is still there hanging on by its rusty hinges and secured with a padlock old and rusted whose key I suspect has long been lost.

As the nights began to draw in our outdoor adventures came to an end except for BONFIRE NIGHT! At that time of the year by the time we arrived home after school it was usually too dark for roving far, so our activities were confined to the weekends. In the run up to the big night we had two pursuits. The first was to make a Guy Fawkes and tour the neighbourhood collecting pennies and half pennies 'for the Guy'. To make him we had to scrounge any old bits of clothes that anyone could spare – it was hard to tell who was the better dressed the Guy or we boys in our so called play clothes. The small sum of money we collected we used to buy fireworks. We were only able to buy rip-raps and sparklers for the rockets were far too expensive.

Our second task was to build the bonfire with the one aim to make it the biggest in the area if not the whole City. At the weekends we spent all our time looking for anything that would burn, in particular old motor car tyres were highly prized; in those days they were very scarce so when we did get one it had to be well hidden until the night the fire was to be lit, otherwise lads from nearby areas would come and take them. We of course would take theirs given half a chance. The great day finally came. Our Guy was placed on top of the pile by the men who then set it alight. Everybody would come out and enjoy the warmth of the blaze. We boys would set off our rip -raps and have great delight in scaring all the young lassies as they jumped and gave loud bangs around their feet. Then out came the potatoes baked in the red hot ashes around the edge of the blaze; they were delicious. When at last the centre core of the fire collapsed and our Guy fell into the flames everyone cheered. As the fire slowly died to a glowing heap of ashes everyone returned to their homes. Winter had arrived with Christmas just around the corner.

Christmas in the 1920s and 30s was a far cry from today's commercially driven spend-spend attitude that seems to start earlier each year. In the weeks following Bonfire Night families started preparing, everyone doing their bit to help – mothers busy in kitchens making Christmas puddings which all the family helped to mix and stir – fathers throwing in one or two threepenny pieces. Children made paper chains to decorate the house. There was an air of excitement among the children wondering what Father Christmas might bring them – they knew there was little money to spare for toys, but they knew he would bring something. That something might well be and often was a doll or a wooden engine, car or boat made by the parents but they were appreciated just as much as a shop bought one and it was just as treasured.

Late on the evening of Christmas Eve the families with whatever small amount of money they had went to the large market at the top of Fore Street Hill where now stands St Georges Hall. The traders there with their unsold vegetables, fruit, meat and poultry would gladly sell it very cheaply rather than have to throw it away.

There was only Grandma and me so I missed out on a lot of the fun that children with brothers and sisters had. I did sometimes go and see the Hamiltons, but they were only girls. I did not really mind, my Grandma was always doing her best for me and I had my books to read. I had only a few but would read and re-read these many times and never tire of them. Just like all the other boys and girls I would wonder what I might find on my bed Christmas morning. I knew that there would be a book from Grandma bought at Woolworths where nothing cost more than sixpence. I also knew there would be something for me from my father. Looking back, as I do now, I only hope he was generous and gave Grandma some money to help ease her worries. Also in my stocking there was the usual orange, some sweets and the traditional piece of coal for luck.

There are two Christmas mornings that remain very clear in my memory.

The first was when waking I found a large parcel at the bottom of the bed. It was a Meccano set, not an ordinary one but a special one with which you could build models of all kinds of aeroplanes. It was a wonderful surprise and I spent many happy hours with it. A few years later on Christmas Eve my Grandma told me that my father had been a day or two before and he had said my present would not be on my bed because it was too big. Instead I was to take a letter to the Cycle & Toy shop in Cowick Street on Christmas Eve and they would give me my present. Grandma gave me the letter and off I went as fast as I could run, at the shop the letter was opened, the note read and I think it also contained some money. The shopkeeper went out through a door and came back with my present. It was A BICYCLE, my first real bicycle, my very own and that coming summer it opened up a whole new world for me.

Following Christmas and the excitement there was the long, cold winter to be faced. I seem to remember it nearly always snowed and often the canal would freeze over with a thin covering of ice. Keeping warm was the main problem. The one fire we had needed to be kept burning day and night. Before going to bed it would be damped down with slack (coal dust), wet tea leaves and any vegetable peelings. The chimney damper was closed to cut off the draught, the fire would then be reduced to a low, smouldering glow, ready to be revived with a few sticks in the morning. Upstairs the beds were piled with extra blankets and hot water bottles. Sometimes the water in these was used to wash with in the morning. Buckets of cold water had to be kept in close to the fire in case the tap in the yard froze. On these cold winter evenings, before going to bed, my Grandma would give me a large mug or bowl of either hot oxo or milk with a thick slice of bread to 'warm me up inside'. I always looked forward to these winter nightcaps and occasionally have one to this very day.

In those days of the 20s and 30s there was no television; wireless was just in its infancy. In the long dark evenings I had my books and my Grandma. It was in these winter evenings that I read stories of adventure, exploration and far-away places, of the sea and ships and of the pirates who roamed those seas. Among my favourites were Robinson Crusoe, Treasure Island, Blackbeard The Pirate, A Coral Island and accounts of famous voyages of people like Captain Cook who explored so many strange and distant lands. Whenever I came to a place in a book that I did not quite understand or wished to know more about I only had to ask my Grandma. She would tell me just what I wanted to know. Often I would sit and listen while she told me stories of the countries she had visited, India and the east, South Africa and in particular Cape Town. I can still hear her telling me that when low clouds gathered on the top of the Table Mountain it would roll over the edge, the local population in the town below said it was just The Gods laying their tablecloth. The desire to travel to see these strange lands was born within me.

Grandma also taught me how to behave when in the company of adults no matter whether they were of a lowly or a high station in life. When in the company of grown-ups I was never to speak or interrupt unless I was spoken to first and then when I did speak I must address the men as Sir and a lady as Madam. Should a lady enter a room politeness dictated that I must rise and stand until she was seated. My manner of speech and grammar were also subject to her tuition and instruction included the correct laying out of a dining table in a gentleman's house or a grand hotel. Good manners and politeness when in the town were also important to her. When travelling on a tram or, in later years a bus, if it was full and a lady came on it was polite for me to stand and offer her my seat. When passing through a door a gentleman should always hold it open allowing the lady to pass through first.

I discovered that being polite had its rewards. One day shortly before Christmas while out with my Grandma she went into Courtneys, a drapers shop, on the corner of Alphington and Cowick Street, to buy a hairnet which she always wore. The shop sold a variety of goods including books one of which caught my eye, I picked it up and read the synopsis and thought how much I would have liked to be able to read it, but I knew my Grandma simply could not afford the price of one shilling (5p today). Although I was unaware of him an elderly well dressed gentleman must have been watching me for when I had placed the book back he came and spoke to me. He asked me several questions: Did I enjoy reading? What kind did I like to read? What books had I read?

My Grandma having made her purchase came for me and he raised his hat and told her how pleased he was to hear how much I enjoyed reading, the kind of books I liked and also how polite I had been. Turning again to me he asked if I would like to have the book I had been looking at, I replied, 'yes sir very much'. He took the book to the counter, paid for it came back and gave it to me, raised his hat and then left the shop. I was overjoyed and after all these years still clearly remember that incident, the book was called A Coral Island.

I was around thirteen when my Grandma became too frail to look after me. Phyllis and her mother did all they could to care for her. I was taken by my parents to Sidmouth to finish my schooling. I said I would tell you of the big debt they felt they owed to her and they were trying to repay that debt as much as they could. It was however not until over forty years later when Phyllis and I were to meet again and marry that she told me the whole story.

My Grandma was known along the canal as Nurse West and people would come to her for help in times of sickness. Phyllis had two younger sisters Beryl who was living in London with an Aunt who was able to pay for her to have a good education and Eileen the youngest of the five sisters. Eileen was never a very strong child, but much loved by her parents. At this moment in time of which I write she was just a few years old and fell ill. She became worse and a Doctor was sent for – he prescribed some medicine but to no avail. Within a short space of a few hours her little body became burning hot and her joints swollen. The Doctor was called again this time he told her parents that she had a fever which he could not explain and he did not think she would survive the night. His advice was to build up the fire, cover her with all the blankets they had and hope it would burn the fever out. This they did as soon as he had left but it seemed the child was slipping away. The parents in despair sent Phyllis to ask Nurse West if she might be able to help. She returned with Phyllis and after a quick examination of little Eileen took charge. Outside it was a dark, bitterly cold winter night but the first thing she did was to open wide the window; she then told them to dampen down the fire while she removed all the blankets that the Doctor had said to put over her. Leaving the sick child with just a light covering she went back to her cottage returning shortly after with a bottle of medicine she made up a little of which she managed to get down the child's throat. She then told the parents there was nothing more that she or anybody could do. All they now had to do was pray and follow her instructions exactly – to keep the window open and the room cold. If or when the fever broke and her body temperature fell – close the window, keep the fire damped down so it just kept the room above freezing and give her a spoonful of the medicine and she would sleep peacefully. In the early hours of the morning all this took place, the fever reached its peak and broke, the crisis was over and when Nurse West came again in the morning Eileen was asleep and on the road to recovery. Phyllis and her mother and family felt they owed my Grandma a great debt for saving the life of their youngest child when others had given up all hope.

As always spring and summer came and with it our freedom to roam and explore. The year that followed the arrival of my first bicycle widened our horizons. Many of my friends had also acquired bikes and we roamed the country lanes for miles around always wondering what lay round the next bend and where it would take us. There was one incident I will not forget and it always makes me smile. There was a section of the tow path that was about a quarter of a mile long; it was also fairly wide so we decided to use it as a race track. Off we set , just as we reached full speed my front wheel touched the back wheel of another bike, I and my bike took off and landed right in the middle of the canal. My bike sank to the bottom. I could swim. I was safe. Some of my friends had cycled on to the council yard and alerted the men who told my Grandma. Others got the lock keepers boat and carrying a very long pole with a large hook on the end rowed down to the spot where I had gone into the water. Meanwhile I had been taken back to the cottage. Looking back now, I think my Grandma was so relieved that I was safe she forgot to give me a telling off but later the council foreman did, at least I think he was the foreman for he was a very stern and big man.

From then on our bike racing on the canal tow path was forbidden. My bicycle was recovered using the long pole and hook mainly undamaged and returned to me with more words of warning as to what would happen if we did it again. When it had dried out and had been given a good clean I resumed exploration of the lanes and byways enjoying the open air with feeling and desire for adventure. We had not forgotten however our financial enterprise of patrolling the canal in the evenings and returning abandoned boats to their owners for a few coppers to spend on sweets or comics.

At twelve and a half I left my school, my friends and that wonderful playground that was our Never Never Land, where our imaginations created whatever we desired and within those creations we could do whatever we wished. I said goodbye to my friends and the canal, the river and my Grandma who had taught me so much. In Sidmouth I now had three sisters, Margaret, Ruby and Mary together with a very young brother John. My school days were over and my working life was soon to begin. My boyhood memories remain with me still – fresh and green.